Change and Grow

Foal to Horse

Acknowledgements: Cover: getty images/Gordon Clayton, getty images/Dorling Kindersley, gettyimages/Gordon Clayton, gettyimages/Ronald Wittek. p1 gettyimages/Eric Landwehr, p2 gettyimages/Joseph Sohm, p3 gettyimages/Gordon Clayton, p4 gettyimages/MIMOTITO, p5 gettyimages/Joseph Sohm, pp6–7 gettyimages/Rawlins - CMSP, p7 gettyimages/Bob Langrish, p8 gettyimages/Richard Ross, p9 gettyimages/Sisse Brimberg, p10 gettyimages/Eric Landwehr, p11 gettyimages/Per Magnus Persson, p12 gettyimages/Tim Graham, p13 gettyimages/Philip Nealey, p14 gettyimages/Diane Macdonald, p15 gettyimages/Dorling Kindersley, p16 gettyimages/Tom Brakefield, p17 gettyimages/Alan and Sandy Carey, p18 gettyimages/Dorling Kindersley, p19 gettyimages/Tariq Dajani, p20 gettyimages/Geoff Brightling, p21 gettyimages/Jason Todd, p22 gettyimages/Andy Crawford and Kit Houghton, p23 gettyimages, p24 gettyimages/Gordon Clayton.

First published by Parragon in 2009

Parragon
Queen Street House
4 Queen Street
Bath BA1 1HE, UK

ISBN 978-1-4075-8043-2

Printed in China

Discovery KIDS

Change and Grow

Foal to Horse

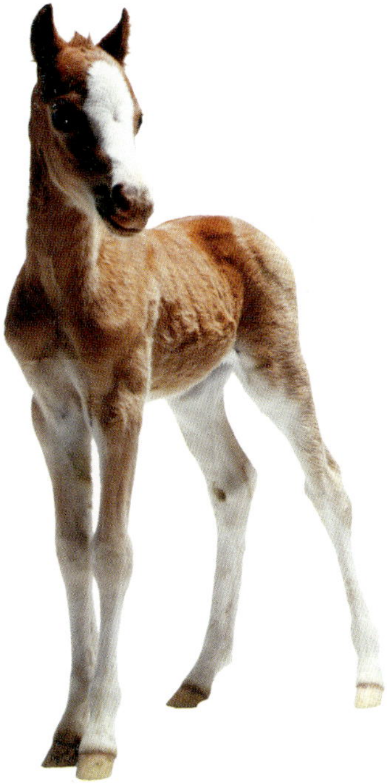

LIVE. LEARN. DISCOVER.

Steve Parker

The Start of Life

It's a fine spring day. The female horse, or mare, is "in season." This means she is ready to mate. She gets together with the male horse, or stallion.

There are more than 200 types of horse—from tiny ponies the size of a pet dog to enormous draft horses.

DiscoveryFact™

A baby begins

After the mare and stallion have mated, a baby horse, or foal, starts to grow inside the mare. It develops in a baglike part of her body called the womb.

Moving on

The stallion does not stay with the mare. She raises her foal alone.

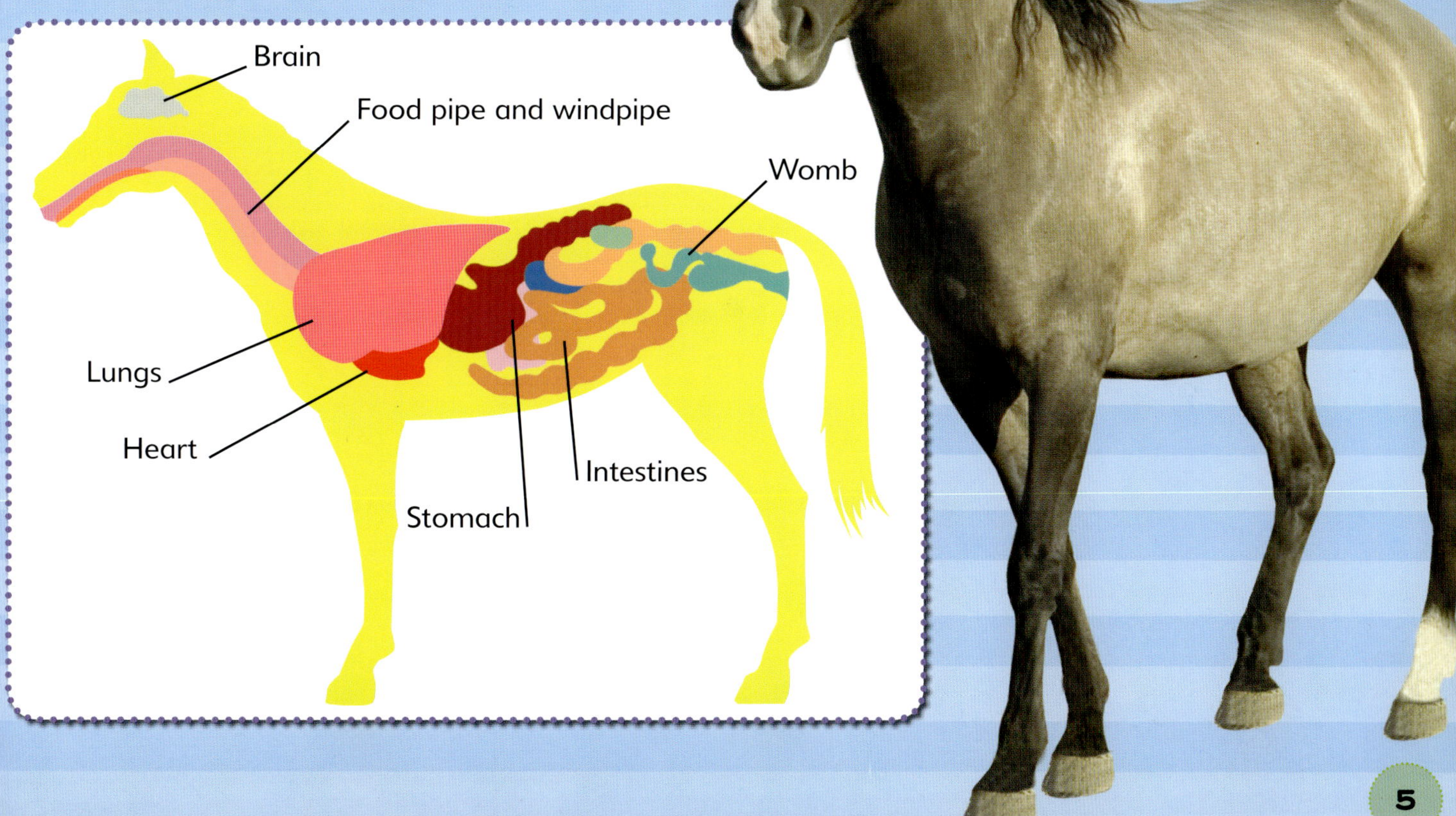

Growing inside

The foal will take 11 months to grow inside its mother's womb. That's two months longer than a human baby.

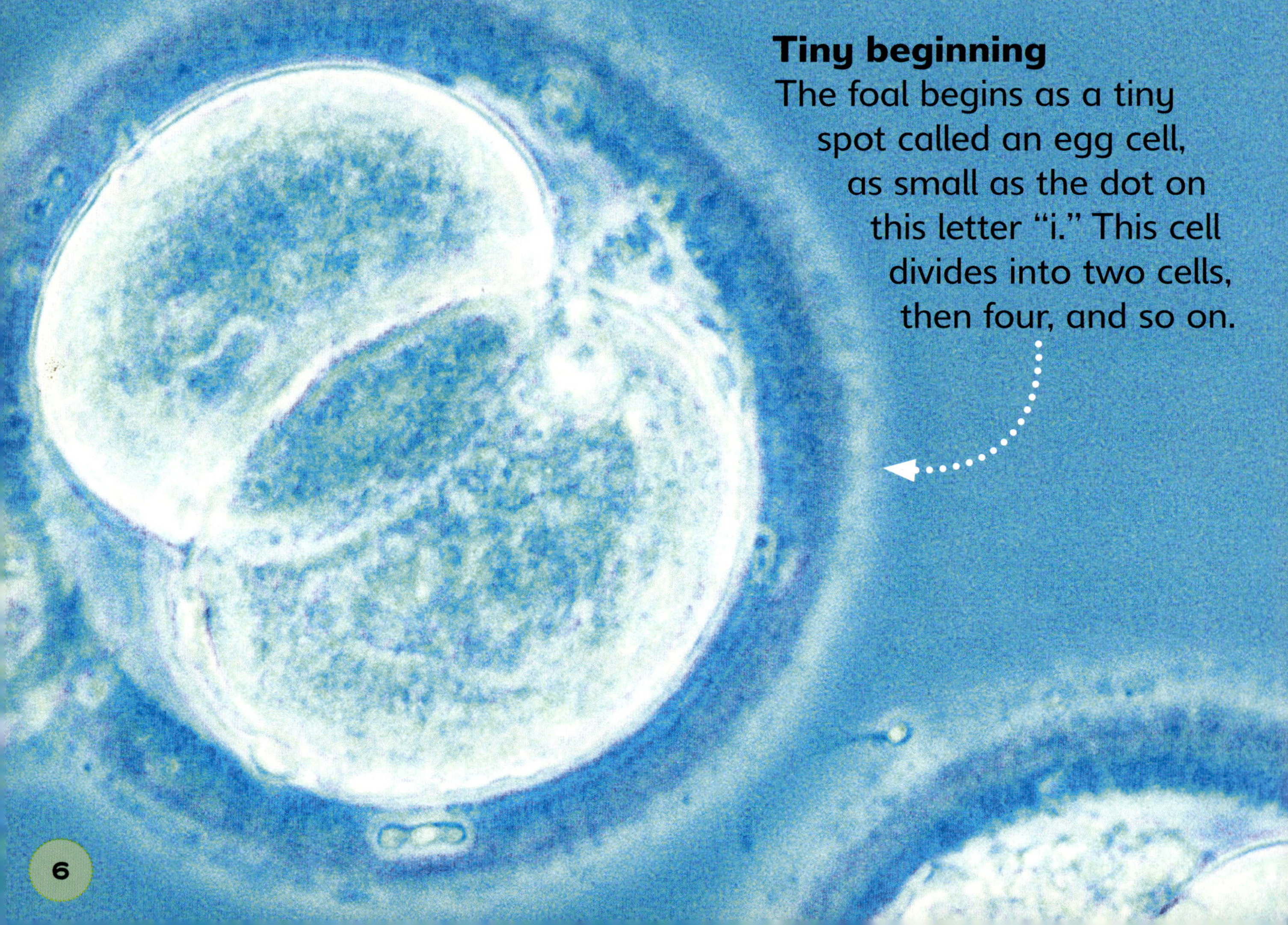

Tiny beginning
The foal begins as a tiny spot called an egg cell, as small as the dot on this letter "i." This cell divides into two cells, then four, and so on.

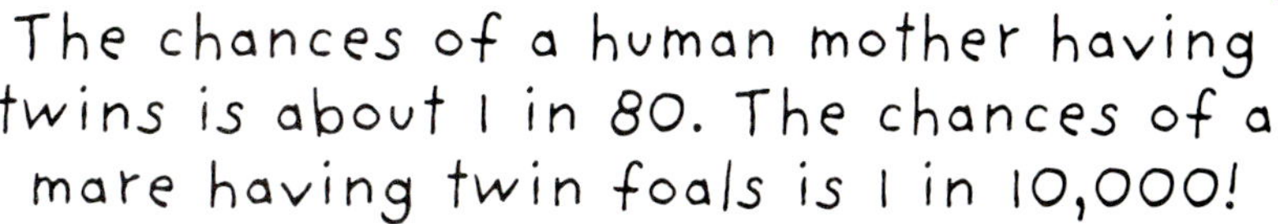

The chances of a human mother having twins is about 1 in 80. The chances of a mare having twin foals is 1 in 10,000!

DiscoveryFact™

Body parts form

After a few weeks the foal is only the size of your fist. But it has all of its body parts, including its nose, ears, eyes, tail—and four legs with tiny hooves.

Expecting

As the foal grows, it curls up inside its mother. Her body stretches and gets bigger to make room for her growing foal.

Here I am!

After 11 months the foal is ready to be born. The mother horse finds a quiet, safe place to lie down.

Ready for birth

Inside the mother horse, the strong muscles of the womb tighten. They squeeze the foal through a gap under the mother's tail called the birth canal.

Front feet first

After a lot of effort the foal is born. Its front feet usually come out first, then its head, body, and back legs. The foal lands softly on the ground.

Most foals are able to stand up and walk about half an hour after birth. It takes a human baby up to a year!

DiscoveryFact™

Clean up

The mother sniffs her foal and nudges it. Then she helps it to stand up.

Mother cleans her foal.

What can I do?

From the moment of birth the foal can see, hear, and smell well. It is soon ready for a drink of its mother's milk.

First food

The foal feels and sniffs for its mother's udder, where the milk is stored. The foal starts to suck milk from the teats.

On the move

Within a few hours, the foal can run quite fast. But its legs seem too long for its body. It sometimes wobbles and falls over.

A newborn foal drinks about 12 pints of milk each day—a human baby drinks less than 2 pints.

DiscoveryFact™

LOTS TO LEARN

The young foal has lots of energy. It trots, gallops, and jumps around. This helps make its bones and muscles grow strong.

The foal uses its sense of smell.

Look and listen

The foal is very alert and aware. It looks and listens to everything around it. It quickly learns about what is safe and what could be harmful.

Safe with Mother
The foal stays close to its mother all the time. She places herself between her foal and any danger. She will kick hard if she feels threatened by anything.

Finding Out

Horses do not sleep all night as we do. Even in the dark the foal can see well. It can also hear noises that are so quiet we cannot hear them.

Testing foods
After about two weeks, the foal's first teeth start to grow. It begins to nibble grass and other plants. It finds out which taste good and which are best to avoid.

Vet check

Soon after the foal is born, a vet (animal doctor) will come to visit it to make sure it is well. It is important that the mother horse knows and trusts the vet.

Horses sleep standing up! The joints in their legs click into place and stop them from falling over.

DiscoveryFact™

The foal has a strong back.

Its legs are strong and straight.

Its feet are clean and healthy.

FOAL FRIENDS

Horses like to be with other horses. A group of horses is called a herd. A few weeks after birth, the foal starts to make friends with other horses.

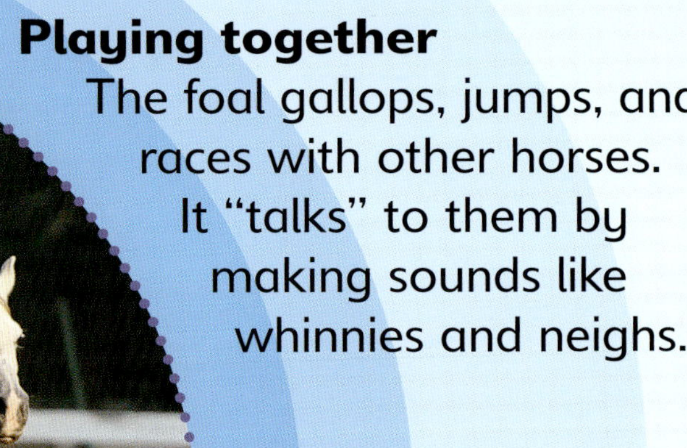

Playing together

The foal gallops, jumps, and races with other horses. It "talks" to them by making sounds like whinnies and neighs.

Body talk

The foal also uses body language to tell others how it feels. If it is happy it sticks its ears straight up. If it is angry it lays its ears flat.

Leader of the herd

No matter how small a herd is, it will probably have a leader—usually an older horse. The foal must learn who is in charge. If it causes trouble it might get a small bite or kick, to show who's boss.

Young foals may rear up as if they are fighting, but they are usually only playing—they may even fall over!

DiscoveryFact™

TIME FOR A CHANGE

The foal is now six months old. It is getting bigger and stronger every day. It is almost time for it to stop feeding on its mother's milk.

Special friends
The foal begins to make special friends in the herd. They graze near each other. As they rest, they nuzzle each other's neck or back.

A female foal is called a filly, and a male foal is called a colt. The coltsfoot flower has leaves shaped like a foal's hooves.

DiscoveryFact™

Testing the leader
As it gets older and braver, the young horse may try to become leader. It may rear up and show its teeth, ready to bite. Or it might kick out.

WORK AND PLAY

It's the young horse's third birthday. It's time for its owners to train it for riding, or maybe for driving.

Going for a ride
The horse may be trained to carry a rider and obey his or her commands.

Experts can tell a horse's age by looking in its mouth! They see how many teeth it has, and how long and worn they are.

DiscoveryFact™

Driving out

The horse may be trained to pull carts, wagons, or carriages. This is called driving. It may also be trained to race, show jump, pull farm machinery—or just look good in the show ring.

ALL GROWN UP

When the horse is four years old it is a full-grown adult. In the next year or two, it may have a foal of its own.

New shoes
The horse needs to wear metal shoes to protect its feet. A farrier fits the horse with new shoes every few months.

Part of the family

The horse may go to a new home. Its owners provide it with a stable or shelter, a field with fresh grass, and extra food. They brush, or groom, their horse often, call the vet if it gets sick—and give it a lot of love and attention.

Most horses live between 20 and 30 years—but "Old Billy" from Manchester, England, lived until he was 62!

DiscoveryFact™

A new foal

As long as the horse is well cared for and has the company of other horses, it will be happy. One day, it may mate and have a foal of its own.

LIFE CYCLE

Mating
The mare and stallion mate.

Pregnancy
The mare becomes pregnant. She will be pregnant for 11 months.

Birth
The foal is born. Almost immediately it stands and drinks milk from its mother.

1–2 days
The foal can now gallop.

1 week
The foal's first teeth begin to grow.

2 weeks
The foal starts to eat grass and other foods besides milk.

2 months
More teeth begin to grow.

4 months
The foal stops feeding on its mother's milk.

1 year
The foal is two-thirds the size of an adult horse and has all its first teeth.

2 years
The young horse may begin to challenge older horses to be leader of the herd.

3–4 years
The horse may be trained for riding or driving.

5 years
The horse is an adult—it has all its adult teeth and is ready to have a foal of its own.